# Life's Reflections

## Piano Solos

## by

## Armen Sahakyan

# Table of Contents

Author Website:

pianistarmensahakyan.com

# Yearning for Serenity

Armen Sahakyan

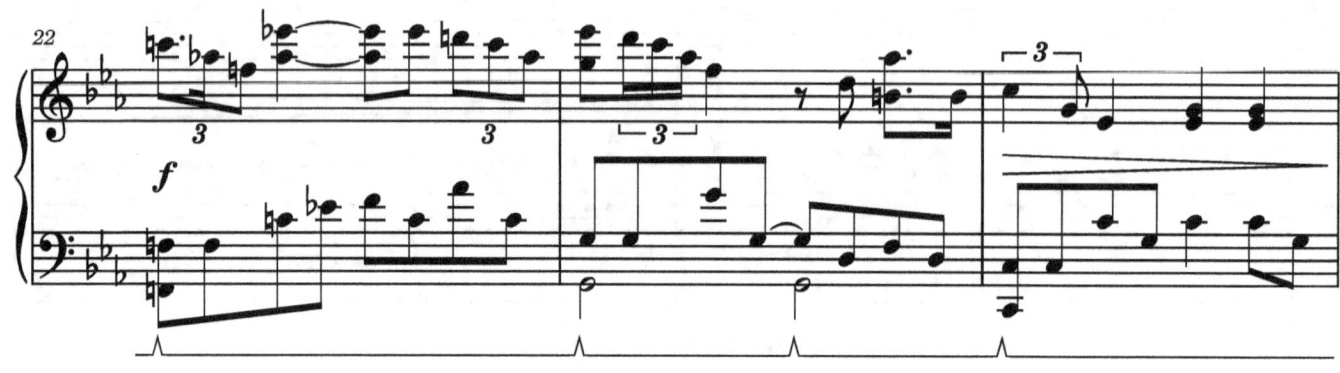

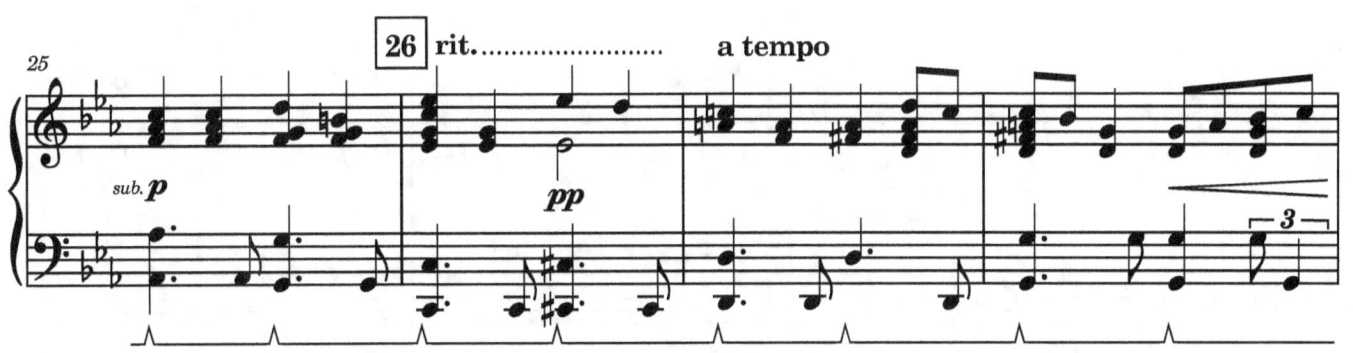

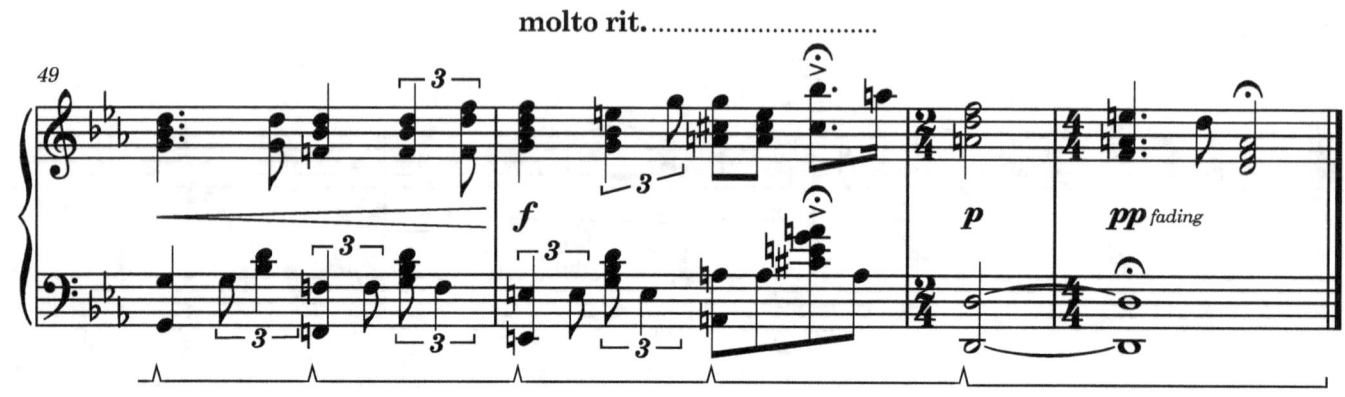

# Glimmer of Hope

Armen Sahakyan

# The Inner Storm

Armen Sahakyan

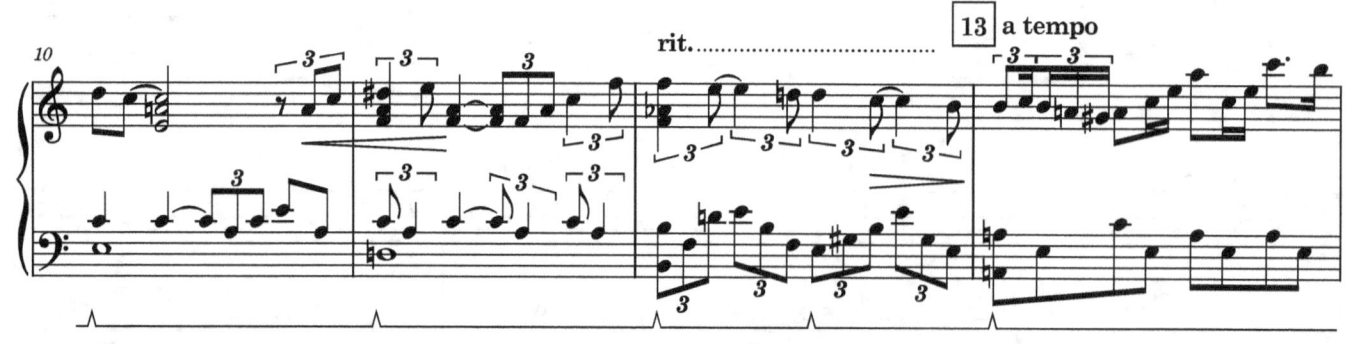

The Inner Storm

13

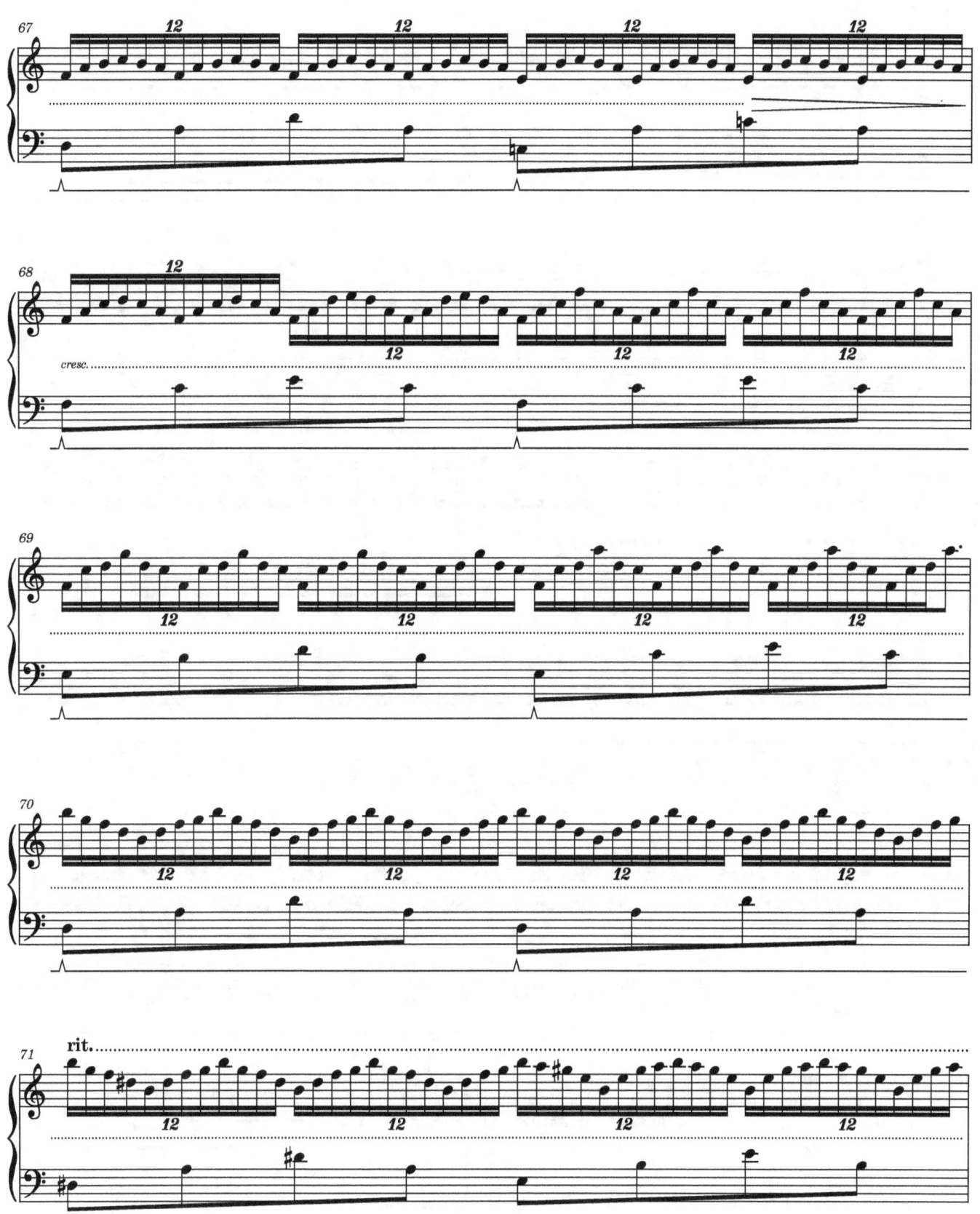

The Inner Storm

15

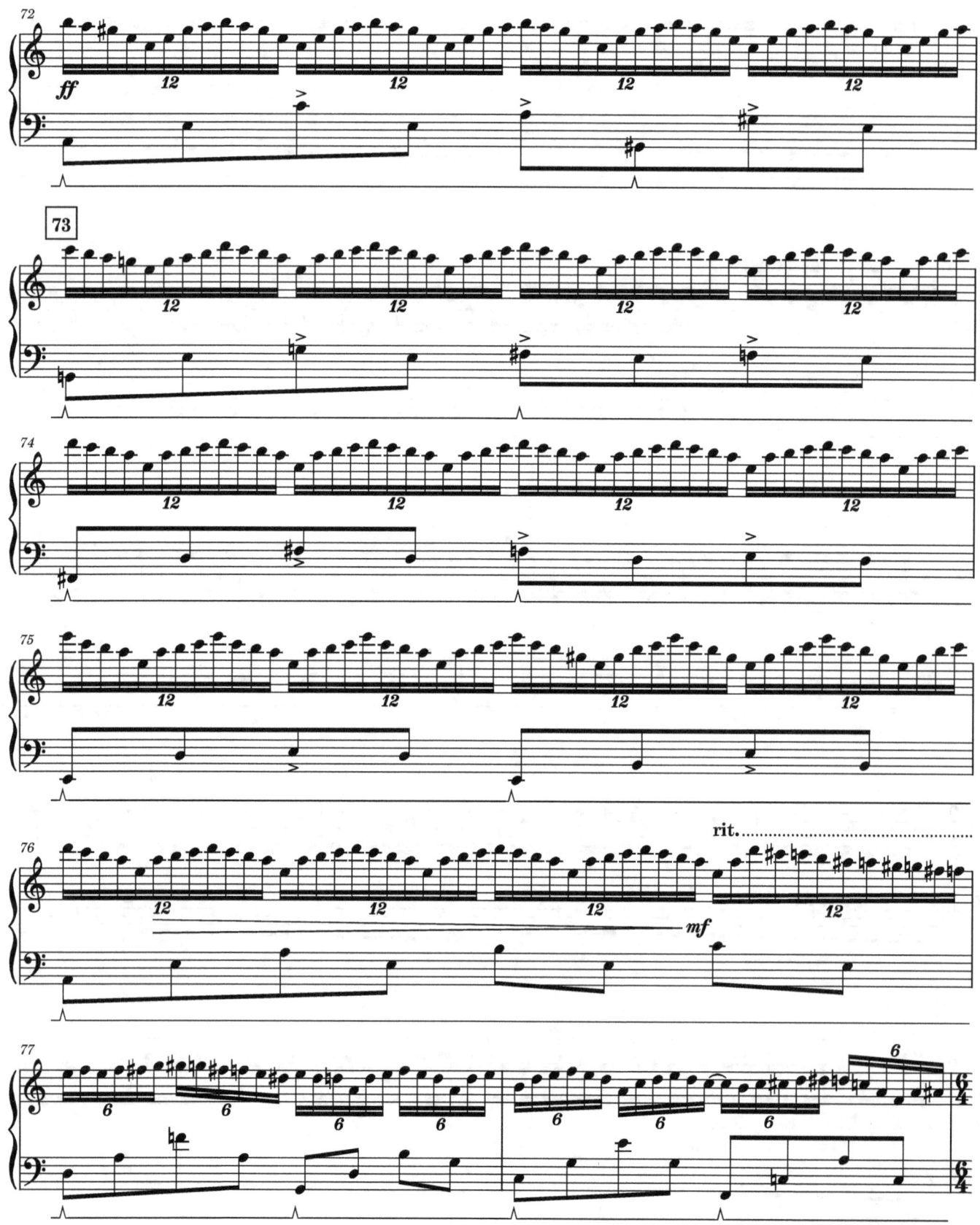

The Inner Storm

# Uncertain Times

Armen Sahakyan

molto rit.

# Burning Desire

Armen Sahakyan

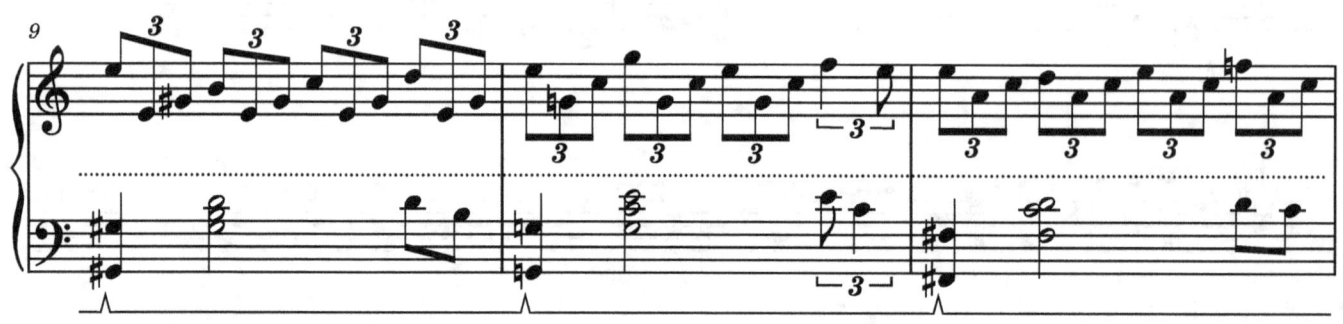

24

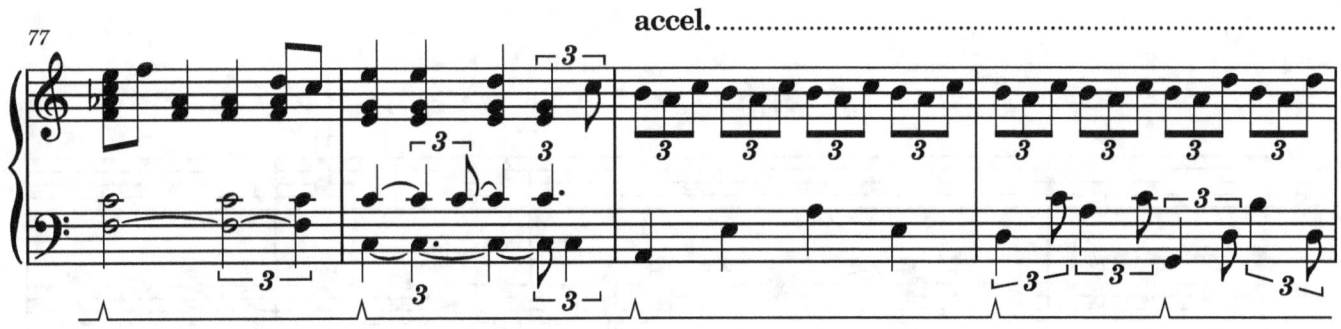

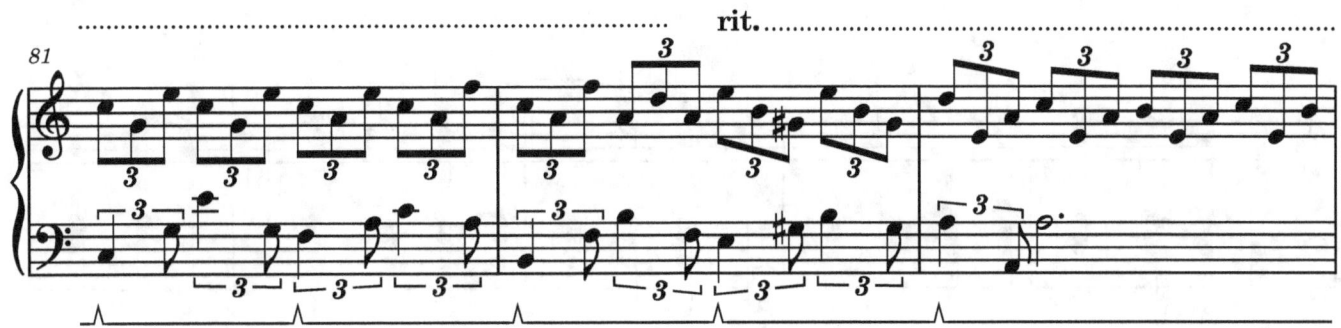

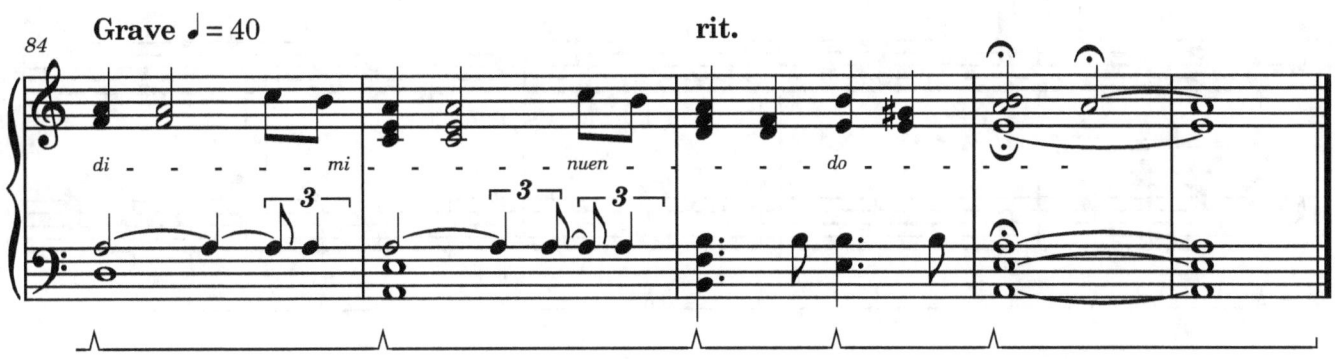

# Forever Last

Armen Sahakyan

30

# New Chapter

Armen Sahakyan

Adagio ♩ = 68

New Chapter

38

# Peaceful Embrace

Armen Sahakyan

Peaceful Embrace

44